Blippi™
Let's Read!

PRE-LEVEL 1: ASPIRING READERS

 LEVEL 1: EARLY READERS
- Easy vocabulary
- Short sentences
- Word repetition
- Simple content and stories reinforced by art

 LEVEL 2: DEVELOPING READERS

 LEVEL 3: ENGAGED READERS

 LEVEL 4: FLUENT READERS

Studio Fun International
An imprint of Printers Row Publishing Group
A division of Readerlink Distribution Services, LLC
9717 Pacific Heights Blvd, San Diego, CA 92121
www.studiofun.com

Blippi™ Copyright ©2022 Moonbug Entertainment. All Rights Reserved.

No part of this publication may be reproduced, distributed, or transmitted in any form or by any means, including photocopying, recording, or other electronic or mechanical methods, without the prior written permission of the publisher, except in the case of brief quotations embodied in critical reviews and certain other noncommercial uses permitted by copyright law.

Printers Row Publishing Group is a division of Readerlink Distribution Services, LLC.
Studio Fun International is a registered trademark of Readerlink Distribution Services, LLC.

All notations of errors or omissions should be addressed to Studio Fun International, Editorial Department, at the above address.

ISBN: 978-0-7944-4969-8
Manufactured, printed, and assembled in Heshan, China.
First Printing, March 2022. LP/03/22
26 25 24 23 22   1 2 3 4 5

CONTENTS

A Pet for Blippi! 5

I Can Drive an Excavator! 37

This Is My Neighborhood! 69

If I Were a Dinosaur! 101

A Pet for Blippi!

Written by Marilyn Easton
Illustrated by Adam Devaney

This is an animal shelter.

Animals who need homes live here.

Come inside with me!

I love pets!

The shelter has a lot of animals.
There are a lot of dogs.

There are big dogs.
There are small dogs.

There are lots of cats, too.

There are kittens.
There are adult cats.

I love cats!

Wow!
Look at all the birds.

Cute little bunnies live here, too.

I love birds and bunnies!

There are turtles here, too.

There are even lizards.

I love turtles and lizards!

These people want a cat.

They play with the cats.

They talk to the cats.

They pet the cats, too.

They find the right cat for them!

The cat has a new family.

That makes me so happy.
I love when pets are adopted!

I hope these dogs get homes, too.

I see one dog by himself.
I will take him on a walk.

Ha, ha, ha!

This dog has an orange bow tie.

I show him my orange bow tie.

He looks like he is laughing.
We are having a happy walk.

This dog has a name tag.
His name is Lyno.

I show Lyno my name tag.

"My name is Blippi!" I say.

Lyno wags his tail.

Next, we play fetch.
We are having fun.

I like Lyno.

Lyno likes me.

I will give Lyno a new home!
I will take good care of him.

I will feed him.

I will brush him.

I will walk him.

I will play with him.

I will take him for checkups.

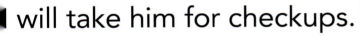

Most of all, I will love him!

"What do you think?" I ask Lyno. "Do you want me to adopt you?"

Lyno says YES.

Lyno and I are a good match.

The shelter agrees.
I can adopt Lyno!

I came to volunteer today.
I am leaving with a new pet!

I love when pets are adopted. Welcome home, Lyno!

I Can Drive an Excavator!

Written by Marilyn Easton
Illustrated by Adam Devaney

Look at this big machine!

It is an excavator.

It is a big machine that digs.

The excavator has a bucket.
The bucket digs in the ground.
The bucket picks up dirt.

The excavator moves the dirt.
Excavators are the best!
I wish I could drive one.

Wow!

My wish just came true.

I can drive an excavator!
It works hard.
I will too.

I have to be safe.

A hard hat goes on my head.

A vest helps people see me.

This is the cab.

It is where I sit.

It is just one step up.

Make that one BIG step!

I put on my seat belt.

Now I can drive!

An excavator has tracks.
It does not have wheels.

The tracks move over mud.
The tracks move over rocks.

The ride is not bumpy.

Thank you, excavator tracks!

It is time to dig!
The bucket is up.

I bring the bucket down.
The bucket digs in the ground.

I lift the bucket.
It is full of dirt.

The excavator is on the move.
Go, excavator, go!

The excavator drives to a truck.
It is a dump truck.

I lower the bucket.

The bucket drops the dirt.

The dirt lands in the dump truck.

Now there is no dirt in the bucket.

The dirt is in the dump truck.

The dump truck drives away with the dirt.
See you later, dirt!

The excavator's work is done.
Good job, excavator!

There are more big machines at work.

Let's look!

A backhoe has two buckets.
There is a bucket in the front.
There is a bucket in the back.

Here comes a crane.
It lifts big and heavy things.

Here comes a truck.

It holds wood and beams.

Slosh! Slosh!

Do you hear that?

This truck mixes concrete.

Check this out.

This is a steamroller.

It flattens the ground.

The big machines work hard.

They build a new playground.
The playground is for you!

This Is My Neighborhood!

Written by Nancy Parent
Illustrated by Maurizio Campidelli

Welcome to my neighborhood.
Come and take a walk with me!

There are houses in my neighborhood

There are apartment buildings, too.

The people in my neighborhood are my neighbors!

First I go to the park.
I like to feed the birds.

The park has trees and a pond.

I love the park.

My neighbors love the park, too.

I walk by the post office.

I mail a letter.

I say hi to the mail person.

I like to say hello to my neighbors.
Do you say hello to your neighbors?

There is a playground where students play.

What do you like to play at the playground?

Firefighters use the fire truck to put out fires.

Firefighters are the best!

I go to the doctor's office.
I have a checkup today.

My neighborhood has a veterinarian, too.

This is where Lyno gets his checkups.

I walk by the police station.

Police officers keep my neighborhood safe.

Now I go to the grocery store.

This is where my neighbors and I buy food.

Wow, I love apples!

What is your favorite food?

I walk by the bakery.
It has sweet things to eat.

Here is the flower shop.

I love flowers!

I go to the barber.
I need a haircut today.

My neighborhood even has a shoe repair store.

Today I got orange shoelaces!

I walk by the laundromat

Clothes spin around and around until they are clean.

Clean clothes are the best!

I go to the neighborhood diner. This sandwich is amazing!

It's time for dessert.

I love my neighborhood ice cream truck.

I go to the library.
There are so many books here!

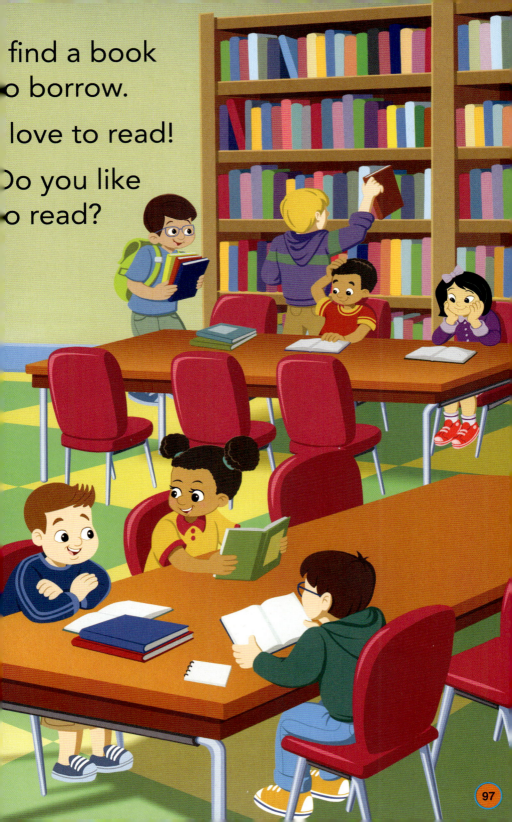

find a book
to borrow.

I love to read!

Do you like
to read?

It is time to pick up Lyno.

He is at the doggy day care center

These doggies are so cute!

I think Lyno is happy to see me.
I am happy to see him!

This is my neighborhood.
Thanks for taking a walk with me!

Blippi

If I Were a Dinosaur!

Written by Meredith Rusu
Illustrated by Adam Devaney

I had a great day.
I went to the dinosaur museum.

I saw big dinosaurs.
I saw small dinosaurs.

I saw scary dinosaurs.
I saw funny dinosaurs, too.

All those dinosaurs made me think.
What if I were a dinosaur?
What kind would I be?

Some dinosaurs had big feet.

I could have big feet.
I could make big footprints.

Some dinosaurs were very tall.

I could be tall, too.

What do you think, Lyno?

Some dinosaurs ran very fast.

I could be a dinosaur like that.

I could run fast.

Some dinosaurs had sharp teeth. They bit through any food.

I could be a dinosaur like that.
I can bite through any food.

Some dinosaurs flew.
Some had big wings.

I could have big wings.
I could fly.

Some dinosaurs had big horns. Triceratops had three horns.

I could have three horns.

Some dinosaurs only ate plants.
Stegosaurus only ate plants.

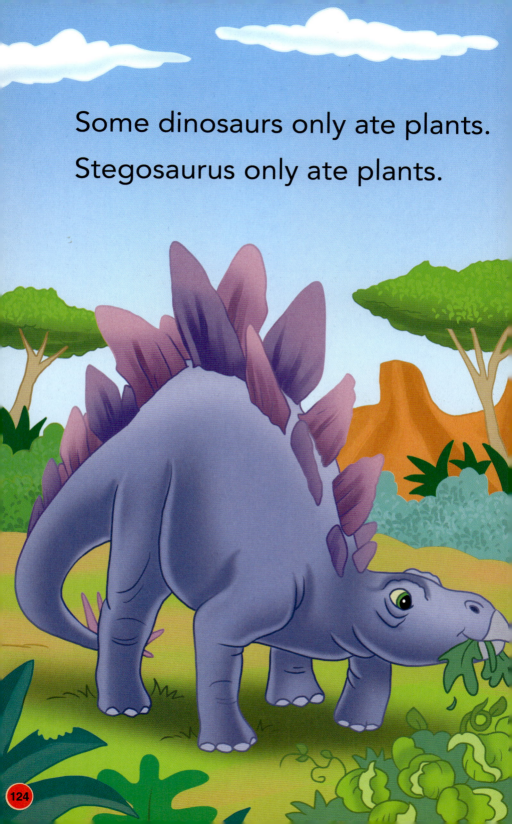

I love my garden.
I could eat only plants!

Dinosaurs hatched from eggs.
The eggs were big.

I could pretend to be in an egg.
I could hatch.
Here I am, world!

Some dinosaurs roared a lot.
Tyrannosaurus rex roared a lot.

It was fun to see dinosaurs.

It was fun to be dinosaurs.

Dinosaurs are amazing.

You are amazing, too!